The
ANTI INFLAMMATORY
COOKBOOK
For Beginners

*easy and delicious recipes
for your
anti inflammatory diet*

Dana F. William

Table of Contents

Table of Contents

Introduction

An anti-inflammatory nutrition is an eating plan that aims to reduce or prevent chronic inflammation in the human body, which can cause many severe medical conditions if left untreated.

This nutrition focuses on fresh vegetables and fruits. Many plant-based foods around us give us antioxidants. It also focuses on nuts, lean proteins, whole grains, healthy fats, spices, and seeds. The intake of alcohol, red meats, and processed foods is discouraged. So you have to avoid them or limit their intake as much as you can. Remember the following:

- Vegetables and fruits have natural components known as phytonutrients, which can protect us against inflammation.
- Foods that have a lot of saturated fats can, on the other hand, increase inflammation. Also, foods containing trans fats and highly processed foods can also be inflammatory to your body.
- Healthy fats like omega-3 fatty acids and monounsaturated fats can help you stay away from chronic inflammation.

Also, make sure to achieve a good balance of carbs, protein, and fat in every meal you have. Your anti-inflammatory eating plan must also meet the requirements of your body by providing you with all the minerals, fiber, vitamins, and water you need. Few simple lifestyle changes can give you many benefits. Change to an anti-inflammatory eating plan, get enough sleep, reduce stress, and exercise. You will certainly see a marked improvement.

- You will see a reduced risk of diabetes, obesity, heart disease, cancer, and depression, among others.
- The symptoms of inflammatory bowel syndrome, arthritis, lupus, and several autoimmune diseases will improve.
- Inflammatory markers in the blood will go down.
- Markers for cholesterol, triglyceride, and blood sugar will improve.
- Your mood and energy levels will go up.

You must eat the right foods to beat chronic inflammation and avoid the diseases it causes. However, consuming only the right food is never going to be enough. You may have to make some lifestyle modifications as well.

This cookbook will help you prepare meals with delicious, easy and above all healthy recipes to maintain a healthy lifestyle!

1. Breakfast Oatmeal

PREPARATION: 5 MIN   COOKING: 8 MIN   SERVES:1

What You Need

- 2/3 cup coconut milk
- 1 egg white, pasture-raised
- ½ cup gluten-free quick-cooking oats
- ½ teaspoon turmeric powder
- ½ teaspoon cinnamon
- ¼ teaspoon ginger

How To Cook

1. Place the non-dairy milk in a saucepan and heat over medium flame.

2. Stir in the egg white and continue whisking until the mixture becomes smooth.

3. Add in the rest of the ingredients and cook for another 3 minutes.

Nutritions

Calories 395, Total Fat 34g, Saturated Fat 7g, Total Carbs 19g, Net Carbs 16g, Protein 10g, Sugar: 2g, Fiber: 3g, Sodium: 76mg, Potassium 459mg

2. Scrambled Eggs with Smoked Salmon

 PREPARATION: 10 MIN   COOKING: 10 MIN   SERVES: 2

What You Need

- 4 eggs
- 2 tablespoons coconut milk
- Fresh chives, chopped
- 4 slices of wild-caught smoked salmon, chopped
- Salt to taste

How To Cook

1. In a bowl, whisk the egg, coconut milk, and chives.

2. Grease the skillet with oil and heat over medium-low heat.

3. Pour the egg mixture and scramble the eggs while cooking. When the eggs start to settle, add in the smoked salmon and cook for 2 more minutes.

Nutritions

Calories 349, Total Fat 23g, Saturated Fat 4g, Total Carbs 3g, Net Carbs 1g, Protein 29g, Sugar 2g, Fiber 2g, Sodium 466mg, Potassium 536mg

3. Choco-Nana Pancakes

 PREPARATION: 5 MIN   COOKING: 6 MIN   SERVES: 2

What You Need

- 2 large bananas, peeled and mashed
- 2 large eggs, pasture-raised
- 3 tablespoon cacao powder
- 2 tablespoons almond butter
- 1 teaspoon pure vanilla extract
- 1/8 teaspoon salt
- Coconut oil for greasing

How To Cook

1. Preheat a skillet on medium-low heat and grease the pan with coconut oil.

2. Place all ingredients in a food processor and pulse until smooth.

3. Pour a batter (about ¼ cup) onto the skillet and form a pancake. Cook for 3 minutes on each side.

Nutritions

Calories 303, Total Fat 17g, Saturated Fat 4g, Total Carbs 36g, Net Carbs 29g, Protein 5g, Sugar 15g, Fiber 5g, Sodium 108mg, Potassium 549mg

4. Raspberry Grapefruit Smoothie

 PREPARATION: 5 MIN   COOKING: 0 MIN   SERVES:1

What You Need

- Juice from 1 grapefruit, freshly squeezed
- 1 banana, peeled and sliced
- 1 cup raspberries

How To Cook

1. Place all ingredients in a blender and pulse until smooth.

2. Chill before serving.

Nutritions

Calories 381, Total Fat 0.8g, Saturated Fat 0.1g, Total Carbs 96g, Net Carbs 85g, Protein 4g, Sugar 61g, Fiber 11g, Sodium 11mg, Potassium 848mg

5. Breakfast Burgers with Avocado Buns

 PREPARATION: 10 MIN   COOKING: 5 MIN   SERVES:1

What You Need

- 1 ripe avocado
- 1 egg, pasture-raised
- 1 red onion slice
- 1 tomato slice 1 lettuce leaf
- Sesame seed for garnish
- Salt to taste

How To Cook

1 Peel the avocado and remove the seed. Slice the avocado into half. This will serve as the bun. Set aside. Grease a skillet over medium flame and fry the egg's sunny side up for 5 minutes or until set.

2 Assemble the breakfast burger by placing on top of one avocado half with the egg, red onion, tomato, and lettuce leaf.

3 Top with the remaining avocado bun. Garnish with sesame seeds on top and season with salt to taste.

Nutritions

Calories 458, Total Fat 39g, Saturated Fat 4g, Total Carbs 20g, Net Carbs 6g, Protein 13g, Sugar 8g, Fiber 14g, Sodium 118mg, Potassium 1184mg

Lunch

6. Buckwheat Noodle Soup

PREPARATION: 10 MIN   COOKING: 25 MIN   SERVES: 4

What You Need

- 2 cups Bok Choy, chopped
- 3 tbsp. Tamari
- 3 bundles of Buckwheat Noodles
- 2 cups Edamame Beans
- 7 oz. Shiitake Mushrooms, chopped
- 4 cups Water
- 1 tsp. Ginger, grated
- Dash of Salt
- 1 Garlic Clove, grated

How To Cook

1 First, place water, ginger, soy sauce, and garlic in a medium-sized pot over medium heat. Bring the ginger-soy sauce mixture to a boil and then stir in the edamame and shiitake to it. Continue cooking for further 7 minutes or until tender.

2 Next, cook the soba noodles by following the Directions: given in the packet until cooked. Wash and drain well. Now, add the bok choy to shiitake mixture and cook for further one minute or until the bok choy is wilted.

3 Finally, divide the soba noodles among the serving bowls and top it with the mushroom mixture.

Nutritions

Calories 234Kcal, Proteins 14.2g, Carbohydrates 35.1g, Fat 4g

7.Chickpea Curry

PREPARATION: 10 MIN   COOKING: 25 MIN   SERVES:4 TO 6

What You Need

- 2 × 15 oz. Chickpeas, washed, drained & cooked
- 2 tbsp. Olive Oil
- 1 tbsp. Turmeric Powder
- ½ of 1 Onion, diced
- 1 tsp. Cayenne, grounded
- 4 Garlic cloves, minced
- 2 tsp. Chili Powder

- 15 oz. Tomato Puree
- Black Pepper, as needed
- 2 tbsp. Tomato Paste
- 1 tsp. Cayenne, grounded
- ½ tbsp. Maple Syrup
- ½ of 15 oz. can of Coconut Milk
- 2 tsp. Cumin, grounded
- 2 tsp. Smoked Paprika

How To Cook

1. Heat a large skillet over medium-high heat. To this, spoon in the oil.

2. Once the oil becomes hot, stir in the onion and cook for 3 to 4 minutes or until softened. Next, spoon in the tomato paste, maple syrup, all seasonings, tomato puree, and garlic into it. Mix well.

3. Then, add the cooked chickpeas to it along with coconut milk, black pepper, and salt. Now, give everything a good stir and allow it to simmer for 8 to 10 minutes or until thickened. Drizzle lime juice over it and garnish with cilantro, if desired.

Nutritions

Calories 224Kcal, Proteins 15.2g, Carbohydrates 32.4g, Fat 7.5g

8. Goat Cheese & Bell Pepper Salad

PREPARATION: 10 MIN

COOKING: 20 MIN

SERVES: 4

What You Need

- 2 tbsp. Lemon Juice, fresh
- 1 ½ Red Bell Pepper, large
- ¾ cup Goat Cheese, crumbled
- 2 tbsp. Extra Virgin Olive Oil
- 1/3 cup Red Onion, chopped

- 1/3 cup Red Onion, chopped
- 1 tbsp. Oregano, fresh & chopped
- 1 ½ cup Celery, diced
- 4 cups Spinach leaves, chopped coarsely

How To Cook

1 First, mix oregano, oil, and lime juice in a small bowl with a whisker until combined well.

2 Next, check for seasoning and spoon in more salt and pepper as needed. Then, stir in the spinach, goat cheese, bell pepper, red onion, and celery in a large bowl.

3 To this, stir in the dressing and toss well. Serve immediately and enjoy it.

Nutritions

Calories 155Kcal, Proteins 5.7g, Carbohydrates 8.8g, Fat 11.5g

9. Carrot Soup

 PREPARATION: 10 MIN   COOKING: 40 MIN   SERVES: 4

What You Need

- 1 cup Butternut Squash, chopped
- 1 tbsp. Olive Oil
- 1 tbsp. Turmeric Powder
- 14 ½ oz. Coconut Milk, light
- 3 cups Carrot, chopped
- 1 Leek, rinsed & sliced
- 1 tbsp. Ginger, grated
- 3 cups Vegetable Broth
- 1 cup Fennel, chopped
- Salt & Pepper, to taste
- 2 cloves of Garlic, minced

How To Cook

1. Start by heating a Dutch oven over medium-high heat. To this, spoon in the oil and then stir in fennel, squash, carrots, and leek. Mix well. Now, sauté it for 4 to 5 minutes or until softened.

2. Next, add turmeric, ginger, pepper, and garlic to it. Cook for another 1 to 2 minutes. Then, pour the broth and coconut milk to it. Combine well. After that, bring the mixture to a boil and cover the Dutch oven. Allow it to simmer for 20 minutes.

3. Once cooked, transfer the mixture to a high-speed blender and blend for 1 to 2 minutes or until you get a creamy smooth soup. Check for seasoning and spoon in more salt and pepper if needed.

Nutritions

Calories 210.4 Kcal, Proteins 2.1g, Carbohydrates 25.6g, Fat 10.9g

10. Herbed Baked Salmon

 PREPARATION: 10 MIN   COOKING: 15 MIN   SERVES: 2

What You Need

- 10 oz. Salmon Fillet
- 1 tsp. Olive Oil
- 1 tsp. Honey
- 1 tsp. Tarragon, fresh

- 1/8 tsp. Salt
- 2 tsp. Dijon Mustard
- ¼ tsp. Thyme, dried
- ¼ tsp. Oregano, dried

How To Cook

1. Preheat the oven to 425 ˚ F. After that, combine all the ingredients, excluding the salmon in a medium-sized bowl.

2. Now, spoon this mixture evenly over the salmon.

3. Then, place the salmon with the skin side down on the parchment paper-lined baking sheet. Finally, bake for 8 minutes or until the fish flakes.

Nutritions

Calories 239Kcal, Proteins 31g, Carbohydrates 3g, Fat 11g

Snacks

11. Cauliflower Hummus

PREPARATION: 10 MIN   COOKING: 0 MIN   SERVES: 4

What You Need

- 1 medium head cauliflower, trimmed and chopped
- 2 garlic cloves, chopped
- 2 tablespoons of almond butter
- 2 tablespoons olive oil
- 1/8 teaspoon ground cumin
- Salt, to taste
- Pinch of cayenne pepper

How To Cook

1 In a large pan with boiling water, add cauliflower and cook for about 4-5 minutes. Remove from heat and drain well. Keep aside to cool it slightly.

2 In a food processor, add cauliflower, butter, cumin, and salt and pulse till smooth.

3 Transfer into a serving bowl. Sprinkle with cayenne pepper and serve immediately.

Nutritions

Calories 213, Total Fat 8.5 g, Saturated Fat 3.1 g, Cholesterol 120 mg, Sodium 497 mg, Total Carbs 21.4 g, Fiber 0 g, Sugar 0 g, Protein 0.1g

12. Green Beans and Avocado with Chopped Cilantro

 PREPARATION: 15 MIN

 COOKING: 10 MIN

 SERVES: 4

What You Need

- Avocados: 2; pitted and peeled
- Green beans - 2/3 pound, trimmed
- Scallions - 5, chopped.
- Olive oil - 3 tablespoons
- A handful cilantro, chopped.
- Salt and black pepper to the taste.

How To Cook

1. Heat up a pan containing oil on a medium-high heat source; then add green beans and stir gently. Cook this mixture for about 4 minutes

2. Add salt and pepper to the pan, and stir gently, then remove the heat and move to a clean bowl. Mix the avocados with salt and pepper and mash with a fork inside a clean bowl.

3. Then add onions and stir properly. Add this over green beans, then toss to ensure it is well coated. Finally, serve with some chopped cilantro on top.

Nutritions

Calories 200, Fat 5g, Fiber 3g, Carbs 4g, Protein 6g

13. Potato Chips

 PREPARATION: 10 MIN   COOKING: 30 MIN   SERVES: 6

What You Need

- 2 gold potatoes, cut into thin rounds
- 1 tablespoon olive oil
- 2 teaspoons garlic, minced

How To Cook

1 In a bowl, combine the French fries while using the oil along with the garlic, toss, spread more than a lined baking sheet.

2 Put inside the oven and bake at 400 degrees F for a half-hour.

3 Divide into bowls and serve.

Nutritions

Calories 200, Fat 3, Fiber 5, Carbs 13

14. Cereal Mix

PREPARATION: 10 MIN   COOKING: 40 MIN   SERVES: 6

What You Need

- 3 tablespoons extra virgin organic olive oil
- 1 teaspoon hot sauce
- ½ teaspoon garlic powder
- ½ teaspoon onion powder
- ½ teaspoon cumin, ground
- A pinch of red pepper cayenne
- 3 cups rice cereal squares
- 1 cup cornflakes
- ½ cup pepitas

How To Cook

1. In a bowl, combine the oil while using the hot sauce, garlic powder, onion powder, cumin, cayenne, rice cereal, cornflakes and pepitas.

2. Toss and spread on the lined baking sheet.

3. Put inside the oven and bake at 350 degrees F for 40 minutes. Divide into bowls and serve as a snack.

Nutritions

Calories 199, Fat 3g, Fiber 4g, Carbs 12g, Protein 5g

15. Avocado Cilantro Detox Dressing

 PREPARATION: 5 MIN   COOKING: 0 MIN   SERVES: 3

What You Need

- 5 tablespoons lemon juice, freshly squeezed
- 1 clove of garlic, chopped
- 1 avocado, pitted and flesh scooped out
- 1 bunch cilantro, chopped
- ¼ teaspoon salt
- ¼ cup water

How To Cook

1. Place all ingredients in a food processor and pulse until well combined.

2. Pulse until creamy.

3. Place in a lidded container and store in the fridge until ready to use. Use on salads and sandwiches.

Nutritions

Calories 114, Fat 10 g, Carbs 8 g, Protein 2 g, Fibe: 5 g

16. Tasty Turkey Baked Balls

PREPARATION: 10 MIN   COOKING: 30 MIN   SERVES: 6

What You Need

- 1 pound ground turkey
- ½-cup fresh breadcrumbs, white or whole wheat
- ½-cup Parmesan cheese, freshly grated
- ½-Tbsp. basil, freshly chopped
- ½-Tbsp. oregano, freshly chopped
- 1-pc large egg, beaten
- 1-Tbsp. parsley, freshly chopped
- 3-Tbsp.s milk or water
- A dash of salt and pepper
- A pinch of freshly grated nutmeg

How To Cook

1 Preheat your oven to 350°F. Line two baking pans with parchment paper. Stir in all of the ingredients in a large mixing bowl.

2 Form 1-inch balls from the mixture and place each ball in the baking pan. Put the pan in the oven.

3 Bake for 30 minutes, or until the turkey cooks through and the surfaces turn brown. Turn the meatballs once halfway into the cooking.

Nutritions

Calories 517, Fat 17.2 g, Protein 38.7 g, Carbs 52.7 g, Fibe: 1 g

17. Feta-Filled & Tomato-Topped Turkey Burger Bites

PREPARATION: 10 MIN   COOKING: 20 MIN   SERVES:1

What You Need

- 1-lb turkey, lean, ground
- ½-tsp black pepper
- Kosher or sea salt to taste
- ½-cup tomatoes, sun-dried, diced
- ½-cup Feta cheese, low fat
- 2-Tbsp.s green onions or chives, diced

How To Cook

1. Stir in all the listed ingredients in a mixing bowl. Mix well until blended thoroughly. Divide the mixture evenly into four patties. Store them in the refrigerator.

2. When cooking time comes, you can either grill or fry the frozen patties for about 10 minutes each on both sides.

3. Serve by topping the burgers with your preferred condiments.

Nutritions

Calories 238, Fat 7.9 g, Protein 17.8 g, Carbs 26.8 g, Fiber 3g

18. Sautéed Shrimp Jambalaya Jumble

 PREPARATION: 15 MIN   COOKING: 30 MIN   SERVES: 4

What You Need

- 10-oz. medium shrimp, peeled
- ¼-cup celery, chopped ½-cup onion, chopped
- 1-Tbsp. oil or butter ¼-tsp garlic, minced
- ¼-tsp onion salt or sea salt
- ⅓-cup tomato sauce ½-tsp smoked paprika
- ½-tsp Worcestershire sauce
- ⅔-cup carrots, chopped
- 1¼-cups chicken sausage, precooked and diced
- 2-cups lentils, soaked overnight and precooked
- 2-cups okra, chopped
- A dash of crushed red pepper and black pepper
- Parmesan cheese, grated for topping (optional)

How To Cook

1. Sauté the shrimp, celery, and onion with oil in a pan placed over medium-high heat for five minutes, or until the shrimp turn pinkish.

2. Add in the rest of the ingredients, and sauté further for 10 minutes, or until the veggies are tender. To serve, divide the jambalaya mixture equally among four serving bowls.

3. Top with pepper and cheese, if desired.

Nutritions

Calories 529, Fat 17.6g, Protein 26.4g, Carbs 98.4g, Fiber 32.3g

19. Ambrosial Avocado & Salmon Salad in Lemon-Dressed Layers

PREPARATION: 10 MIN   COOKING: 0 MIN   SERVES: 4

What You Need

- 6-oz wild salmon 4-units jars
- 1-pc avocado, pitted, peeled, and diced
- 2-cups loosely packed salad greens
- ½-cup Monterey Jack cheese, reduced-fat, shredded
- ¾-cup tomato, chopped

- 1 Tbsp. lemon juice, freshly squeezed
- 1 Tbsp. olive oil, extra-virgin
- 1 tsp honey
- ⅛-tsp Kosher or sea salt
- ⅛-tsp black pepper
- ½-tsp Dijon mustard

How To Cook

1. Combine and whisk all the dressing ingredients, excluding the olive oil in a small mixing bowl. Mix well. Drizzle gradually with the oil into the dressing mixture, and keep whisking while pouring. Pour the dressing as to distribute evenly into each jar.

2. Distribute uniformly into each jar similar amounts of the following ingredients in this order: diced tomatoes, cheese, avocado, salmon, and lettuce.

3. Secure each jar by with its lid, and chill the jars in the fridge until ready for serving.

Nutritions

Calories: 267 Fat: 7.4g Protein: 16.6g Carbs: 38.1g Fiber: 4.8g

20. Zesty Zucchini & Chicken In Classic Santa Fe Stir-Fry

PREPARATION: 5 MIN

COOKING: 15 MIN

SERVES:2

What You Need

- 1-Tbsp. olive oil
- 2-pcs chicken breasts, sliced
- 1-pc onion, small, diced
- 2-cloves garlic, minced 1-pc zucchini, diced
- ½- cup carrots, shredded
- 1-tsp paprika, smoked 1-tsp cumin, ground
- ½-tsp chili powder ¼-tsp sea salt
- 2-Tbsp. fresh lime juice
- ¼-cup cilantro, freshly chopped
- Brown rice or quinoa, when serving

How To Cook

1 Sauté the chicken with olive oil for about 3 minutes until the chicken turns brown. Set aside. Use the same wok and add the onion and garlic. Cook until the onion is tender. Add in the carrots and zucchini.

2 Stir the mixture, and cook further for about a minute. Add all the seasonings into the mix, and stir to cook for another minute. Return the chicken in the wok, and pour in the lime juice.

3 Stir to cook until everything cooks through. To serve, place the mixture over cooked rice or quinoa and top with the freshly chopped cilantro.

Nutritions

Calories 191, Fat 5.3g, Protein 11.9g, Carbs 26.3g, Fiber 2.5g

Soups

21. Green Enchiladas Chicken Soup

What You Need

- 2½ lbs. chicken thighs or breasts, skinless or boneless
- 24 oz. chicken broth
- 28 oz. green enchilada sauce
- 1 oz. green salsa
- 1 oz. cubed cream cheese, room temp
- Monterey Jack cheese
- Pepper and salt to taste

How To Cook

1 Place chicken, chicken broth, and green enchilada sauce into a slow cooker.   Cook for about 6-8 hours on low. Remove the chicken and shred it.

2 Scoop 1-2 ladles soup into a bowl then stir in half and half. Place back into the slow cooker.   Add shredded chicken, green salsa, cream cheese, and jack cheese. Turn your slow cooker to warm, then stir for cheeses to melt.

3 Add more salsa or hot sauce to taste.   Top with topping of choice i.e. cilantro, avocado, sour cream, or green onion.

Nutritions

Calories 328, Fats 19.7g, Carbs 6g, Protein 30.8g, Sugars 2.8g, Fiber 0.5g, Sodium 690mg, Potassium 528mg

22. Beef Vegetable Soup

PREPARATION: 20 MIN COOKING: 3 HOURS   SERVES: 6

What You Need

- 1 tbsp. divided avocado or olive oil
- Minced garlic cloves
- ¾ tbsp. thyme, dried
- 1½ tbsp. basil, dried
- 1 tbsp. oregano, dried
- ½ tbsp. black pepper, ground
- ¾ tbsp. sea salt
- 1½ lbs. beef Steak or stew beef, chopped to small pieces
- 1 small chopped onion
- 1 chopped red bell pepper
- Chopped celery stalks
- 1x 798ml can tomatoes, diced
- ½ lb. trimmed green beans, chopped
- 2 cups beef broth or beef bone stock

How To Cook

1 Heat 1 tbsp. oil in a skillet over medium-high heat.   Meanwhile, combine garlic, thyme, basil, oregano, black pepper, and salt in a bowl, medium, then set aside.

2 Mix beef and herb blend then sear in the skillet for about 1-2 minutes until golden brown edges.   Transfer the beef into a slow cooker.   Fry onion, pepper, and celery with the remaining oil in the same skillet until onion becomes translucent.

3 Transfer veggies into your slow cooker then add tomatoes, green beans, and beef stock. Stir to mix. Cook for about 3-4 hours on high or 5-6 hours on low.   Season with pepper and salt to taste.   Serve and enjoy.

Nutritions

Calories 424, Total Fat 27.7g, Total Carbs 11.7g, Protein 33.8g, Sugars 4.5g, Fiber 4.7g, Sodium 1421mg, Potassium 1315mg

23. Broccoli Cheese Soup

PREPARATION: 10 MIN   COOKING: 3 HOURS   SERVES:12

What You Need

- 1 tbsp. softened butter, unsalted
- 5 oz cream cheese, softened
- 1 cup whipping cream
- 2 cups of chicken broth (warmed in microwave)
- ½ cup Parmesan cheese

- 2 cups fresh broccoli, chopped
- Dash of thyme
- 2 ½ cups cheddar cheese, shredded
- Salt and pepper to taste

How To Cook

1 In the slow cooker, add butter, cream cheese, whipping cream, chicken broth, water and stir well. When perfectly mixed pour in the Parmesan cheese. In the cooker, add chopped broccoli and thyme.

2 Cover the cooker and cook on low for 3 hours. Perfectly mix the soup, then add cheddar cheese and mix for a while for the cheddar cheese to melt fully.

3 Add salt and pepper to taste. When fully mixed, thin out the soup by adding some water or chicken broth. Serve and enjoy!

Nutritions

Calories 230, Total Fat 20g, Total Carbs 3.8g, Protein 9.8, Sugar 0.9g, Fiber 1g, Sodium 370mg

24. Chicken Chili Soup

PREPARATION: 5 MIN   COOKING: 6 HOURS   SERVES: 8

What You Need

- 2 tbsp. butter, unsalted,
- 1 pepper
- 1 onion
- 1 tbsp. thyme
- 5 chicken thighs
- 8 pieces of bacon, sliced,
- 1 tbsp. coconut flour
- 1 tbsp. garlic, minced,

- 1 tbsp. salt
- 1 tbsp. pepper
- 1 cup chicken stock
- 2 tbsp. lemon juice
- ¼ cup coconut milk, unsweetened
- 2 tbsp. tomato paste

How To Cook

1. Place butter pats at the center of your slow cooker.   Thinly dice peppers and onions then disperse them evenly on the bottom of your slow cooker.   Cover with chicken thighs.

2. Distribute your bacon slices over the chicken.   Add coconut flour, garlic, salt, and pepper.

3. Pour in chicken stock, lemon juice, coconut milk, and tomato paste. Cook for 6 hours on low. Breakup chicken, stir, then serve and enjoy.

Nutritions

Calories 470, Fat 38g, Carbs 6g, Protein 27g, Sugar 2g, Fiber 1g, Sodium 720mg, Potassium 460mg

25. Stuffed Pepper Soup

PREPARATION: 15 MIN   COOKING: 8 HOURS   SERVES: 8

What You Need

- 1 lb. ground beef
- 2 tbsp. onion, dried and minced
- 1 tbsp. garlic, minced
- Salt and pepper to taste
- 3 cups beef broth
- 24 oz. marinara sauce

- 1 cup rice cauliflower
- 2 cups chopped bell pepper
- ½ tbsp. oregano
- ½ tbsp. basil
- Shredded mozzarella

How To Cook

1. Sauté the beef, garlic, and onion in a skillet until browned then transfer to a slow cooker. Stir in salt and pepper, beef broth, marinara sauce, riced cauliflower, bell pepper, oregano, and basil to the slow cooker.

2. Cover the slow cooker and cook for 8 hours. Garnish with shredded mozzarella.

3. Serve and enjoy.

Nutritions

Calories 193, Fat 12g, Carbs 9g, Protein 13g, Sugar 6g, Fiber 3g, Sodium 826mg, Potassium 642g

Sides

26. Rice and Beans

PREPARATION: 10 MIN   COOKING: 1 HOUR   SERVES:6

What You Need

- 1 tablespoon olive oil
- 1 yellow onion, chopped
- 2 celery stalks, chopped
- 2 garlic cloves, minced
- 2 cups brown rice

- 1 tablespoon olive oil
- 1 yellow onion, chopped
- 2 celery stalks, chopped
- 2 garlic cloves, minced
- 2 cups brown rice

How To Cook

1 Heat up a pan with the olive oil over medium heat, add celery and onion. Stir and cook for 8 minutes.

2 Add beans and garlic, stir again and sauté them as well for about 5 minutes.

3 Add rice, stock, salt and pepper. Stir, cover, cook for 45 minutes, then divide between plates and serve.

Nutritions

Calories 212, Fat 3g, Fiber 2g, Carbs 2g, Protein 1g

27. Baked Asparagus

 PREPARATION: 10 MIN   COOKING: 15 MIN   SERVES:4

What You Need

- 5 tablespoons olive oil
- 4 garlic cloves, minced
- 2 tablespoons chopped shallot
- Black pepper to the taste
- 1½ teaspoons balsamic vinegar
- 1½ pound asparagus, trimmed

How To Cook

1. Spread the asparagus on a lined baking sheet, and drizzle the oil.

2. Add the garlic, shallot, vinegar and black pepper, then toss well and place in the oven. Bake at 450 degrees F for 15 minutes.

3. Divide between plates and serve as a side dish.

Nutritions

Calories 132, Fat 1g, Fiber 2g, Carbs 4g, Protein 4g

28. Glazed Baby Carrots

 PREPARATION: 10 MIN   COOKING: 15 MIN   SERVES:4

What You Need

- 1 tablespoon olive oil
- 3 pounds baby carrots, peeled
- 1 tablespoon maple syrup
- 1 teaspoon thyme, dried
- 1 tablespoon mustard
- 2 tablespoons veggie stock

How To Cook

1 Heat up a pan with the oil over medium heat, add the baby carrots and brown them for 5-6 minutes.

2 Add the maple syrup, thyme, stock and mustard, mix and cook for 10 minutes more.

3 Divide between plates and serve.

Nutritions

Calories 180, Fat 6g, Fiber 7g, Carbs 15g, Protein 6g

Desserts

29. Blueberry-Peach Cobbler

PREPARATION: 15 MIN   COOKING: 2 HOURS   SERVES:4

What You Need

- 5 tablespoons coconut oil, divided
- 3 large peaches, peeled and sliced
- 2 cups frozen blueberries
- 1 cup almond flour
- 1 cup rolled oats

- 1 tablespoon maple syrup
- 1 tablespoon coconut sugar
- 1 teaspoon ground cinnamon
- ½ teaspoon vanilla extract
- Pinch ground nutmeg

How To Cook

1. Coat the bottom of your slow cooker with 1 tablespoon of coconut oil. Arrange the peaches and blueberries along the bottom of the slow cooker.

2. In a small bowl, stir together the almond flour, oats, remaining 4 tablespoons of coconut oil, maple syrup, coconut sugar, cinnamon, vanilla, and nutmeg until a coarse mixture forms.

3. Gently crumble the topping over the fruit in the slow cooker.Cover the cooker and set to high. Cook for 2 hours and serve.

Nutritions

Calories 180, Fat 6g, Fiber 7g, Carbs 15g, Protein 6g.

30. Chai Spice Baked Apples

 PREPARATION: 15 MIN COOKING: 3 HOURS SERVES:5

What You Need

- 5 apples
- ½ cup water
- ½ cup crushed pecans (optional)
- ¼ cup melted coconut oil
- 1 teaspoon ground cinnamon
- ½ teaspoon ground ginger
- ¼ teaspoon ground cardamom
- ¼ teaspoon ground cloves

How To Cook

1. Core each apple, and peel off a thin strip from the top of each.Add the water to the slow cooker. Gently place each apple upright along the bottom.

2. IIn a small bowl, stir together the pecans (if using), coconut oil, cinnamon, ginger, cardamom, and cloves. Drizzle the mixture over the tops of the apples.

3. Cover the cooker and set to high. Cook for 2 to 3 hours, until the apples soften, and serve.

Nutritions

Calories 217, Fat 12g, Carbs 30g, Sugar 22g, Fiber 6g

31. Cacao Brownies

PREPARATION: 15 MIN   COOKING: 3 HOURS   SERVES:4

What You Need

- 3 tablespoons coconut oil, divided
- 1 cup almond butter
- 1 cup unsweetened cacao powder
- ½ cup coconut sugar
- 2 large eggs2 ripe bananas
- 2 teaspoons vanilla extract
- 1 teaspoon baking soda
- ½ teaspoon sea salt

How To Cook

1 Coat the bottom of the slow cooker with 1 tablespoon of coconut oil.In a medium bowl, combine the almond butter, cacao powder, coconut sugar, eggs, bananas, vanilla, baking soda, and salt

2 Mash the bananas and stir well until a batter forms. Pour the batter into the slow cooker.

3 Cover the cooker and set to low. Cook for 2½ to 3 hours, until firm to a light touch but still gooey in the middle, and serve.

Nutritions

Calories 779, Total Fat 51g, Total Carbs 68g, Sugar 35g, Fiber 15g, Protein 18g, Sodium 665mg

32. Missouri Haystack Cookies

PREPARATION: 15 MIN   COOKING: 1 1/2 HOURS   SERVES:24 pieces

What You Need

- ½ cup coconut oil
- ½ cup unsweetened almond milk
- 1 overripe banana, mashed well
- ½ cup coconut sugar
- ¼ cup cacao powder
- 1 teaspoon vanilla extract
- ¼ teaspoon sea salt
- 3 cups rolled oats
- ½ cup almond butter

How To Cook

1. In a medium bowl, stir together the coconut oil, almond milk, mashed banana, coconut sugar, cacao powder, vanilla, and salt. Pour the mixture into the slow cooker.Pour the oats on top without stirring.

2. Put the almond butter on top of the oats without stirring.Cover the cooker and set to high. Cook for 1½ hours.

3. Stir the mixture well. As it cools, scoop tablespoon-size balls out and press onto a baking sheet to continue to cool. Serve when hardened. Keep leftovers refrigerated in an airtight container for up to 1 week.

Nutritions

Calories 779, Total Fat 51g, Total Carbs 68g, Sugar 35g, Fiber 15g, Protein 18g, Sodium 665mg

33. Coconut-Vanilla Yogurt

PREPARATION: 15 MIN   COOKING: 2 HOURS   SERVES: 3 1/2 cups

What You Need

- 3 (13.5-ounce) cans full-fat coconut milk
- 5 probiotic capsules (not pills)
- 1 teaspoon raw honey
- ½ teaspoon vanilla extract

How To Cook

1. Pour the coconut milk into the slow cooker.Cover the cooker and set to high. Cook for 1 to 2 hours, until the temperature of the milk reaches 180°F measured with a candy thermometer.

2. Turn off the slow cooker and allow the temperature of the milk to come down close to 100°F.Open the probiotic capsules and pour in the contents, along with the honey and vanilla. Stir well to combine.Re-cover the slow cooker, turn it off and unplug it, and wrap it in an insulating towel to keep warm overnight as it ferments

3. Pour the yogurt into sterilized jars and refrigerate. The yogurt should thicken slightly in the refrigerator, where it will keep for up to 1 week.

Nutritions

Calories 305, Total Fat 30g, Total Carbs 7g, Sugar 3g, Fiber 0g, Protein 2g, Sodium 43mg

Salads

34. Chili Cauliflower Rice

PREPARATION: 10 MIN   COOKING: 20 MIN   SERVES:6

What You Need

- 1 cup chopped yellow onion
- 3 tablespoons olive oil
- 2 cups riced cauliflower
- ¾ cup crushed tomatoes
- 2 garlic cloves, minced
- 2 cups veggie stock
- ¼ cup chopped cilantro
- ½ teaspoon chili powder

How To Cook

1. Heat up a pan with the oil over medium-high heat and add the onions and garlic. Stir and cook for 4 minutes.

2. Add cauliflower rice, stock, salt, pepper tomatoes and chili powder then stir, cook for 15 minutes and take off the heat.

3. Add the cilantro and mix briefly, then divide between plates and serve. Enjoy!

Nutritions

Calories 200, Fat 4g, Fiber 3g, Carbs 6g, Protein 8g

35. Black Beans and Veggie Mix

PREPARATION: 10 MIN

COOKING: 1 HOUR

SERVES: 6

What You Need

- 1 teaspoon olive oil
- 16 ounces black beans, soaked and drained
- 12 ounces green bell pepper, chopped
- 12 ounces sweet onion, chopped
- 4 garlic cloves, minced
- 2 ½ teaspoons ground cumin
- 2 tablespoons tomato paste
- 2 quarts water
- A pinch of salt and black pepper

How To Cook

1. Heat up a pot with the oil over medium-high heat and add the onion, bell pepper and garlic. Stir and cook for 5 minutes.

2. Add the beans, cumin, tomato paste, salt, pepper and the water. Toss, bring to a simmer, reduce heat to medium and cook the beans mix for 1 hour.

3. Divide between plates and serve as a side dish.

Nutritions

Calories 221, Fat 5g, Fiber 4g, Carbs 9g, Protein 11g

36. Green Beans and Mushroom Sauté

 PREPARATION: 10 MIN COOKING: 25 MIN SERVES: 6

What You Need

- 1 pound green beans, trimmed
- 8 ounces white mushrooms, sliced
- 1 yellow onion, chopped
- 2 tablespoons olive oil
- ½ cup veggie stock
- A pinch of salt and black pepper

How To Cook

1. Heat up a big pan with the oil over medium-high heat and add the onion, stir and cook for 4 minutes.

2. Add the stock and the mushrooms, then stir and cook for 6 minutes more. Add green beans, salt and pepper.

3. Toss and cook over medium heat for 15 minutes, then divide everything between plates and serve as a side dish.

Nutritions

Calories 182, Fat 4g, Fiber 5g, Carbs 6g, Protein 8g

37. Creamy Rice

 PREPARATION: 10 MIN COOKING: 20 MIN SERVES:4

What You Need

- 14 ounces coconut milk
- 1½ cups jasmine rice
- 1 tablespoon coconut cream
- ½ cup water
- A pinch of salt and white pepper

How To Cook

1. In a pot, mix the rice with the coconut milk, coconut cream, water, salt and white pepper.

2. Stir and bring to a simmer over medium heat for 20 minutes.

3. Stir one more time then divide between plates and serve as a side dish.

Nutritions

Calories 191, Fat 5g, Fiber 4g, Carbs 11g, Protein 9g

38.Simple Broccoli Stir-Fry

 PREPARATION: 10 MIN   COOKING: 12 MIN   SERVES:4

What You Need

- 6 garlic cloves, minced
- 1 broccoli head, florets separated
- ½ cup veggie stock
- 1 tablespoon olive oil
- 1 tablespoon balsamic vinegar
- A pinch of salt and black pepper

How To Cook

1. Heat up a pan with the oil over medium heat, add the garlic, stir and cook for 5 minutes.

2. Add the broccoli, stock, vinegar, salt and pepper.

3. Mix and cook for 7-8 minutes more, then divide between plates and serve as a side dish.

Nutritions

Calories 182, Fat 6g, Fiber 3g, Carbs 8g, Protein 6g

Drinks and Smoothies

39. Berry Smoothie

 PREPARATION: 5 MIN  COOKING: 0 MIN SERVES:2

What You Need

- 300ml Cups Apple
- 1 Banana
- 350g Frozen Berries
- 170g Sour Yoghurt
- 1 Tbsp. Honey
- Berries

How To Cook

1. Mix everything in a blender except the berries until smooth. Garnish with fresh berries.

Nutritions

Calories 221kcal, Carbohydrates 52g, Protein 6g, Fat 1g

40. Pineapple Turmeric Smoothie

 PREPARATION: 5 MIN   COOKING: 0 MIN   SERVES: 2

What You Need

- 1 Banana
- 400g Frozen Pineapple
- 1/4 Cup Coconut Milk
- 1/4 Tbsp. Turmeric Powder

How To Cook

1. Blend everything. Garnish with lemon zest.

Nutritions

Calories 327 kcal, Carbs 48 g, Fat 14 g, Protein 2 g

41. Avocado Smoothie

PREPARATION: 5 MIN   COOKING: 0 MIN   SERVES: 2

What You Need

- 1 Large Avocado (Peeled)
- 1 Cup Golden Milk
- 1/8 Tbsp. Vanilla Extract
- 2 Tbsp. Maple Syrup
- Salt

How To Cook

1 Blend everything. Add ice cubes.

Nutritions

Calories 323.2 kcal, Carbs 29.2 g, Fat 25.1 g, Protein 5.1 g

42. Apple Smoothie

 PREPARATION: 5 MIN   COOKING: 0 MIN   SERVES:2

What You Need

- 2 Cup Apple (Chopped)
- 200ml Sour Yoghurt
- 1/2 Cup Frozen Banana (Chopped)
- 1 Tbsp. Maple Syrup
- 1/8 Tbsp. Cinnamon Powder
- 3/4 Ice Cubes
- Mint Leaves

How To Cook

1 Blend everything. Add ice cubes.

Nutritions

Calories 305 kcal, Carbs 53 g, Fat 2 g, Protein 6 g

43. Papaya Smoothie

 PREPARATION: 5 MIN  COOKING: 0 MIN SERVES: 2

What You Need

- 250ml Golden Milk
- 200gm Ripe Papaya Puree
- 1/8 Tbsp. Cinnamon Powder
- 1 Cup Frozen Banana (Chopped)
- 1 Cup Plain Yoghurt
- 1 Tbsp. Lemon Juice

How To Cook

1. Blend everything and serve.

Nutritions

Calories 224.5 kcal, Carbs 33.7 g, Fat 7.7g, Protein 6.9 g

44. Green Smoothie

PREPARATION: 5 MIN   COOKING: 0 MIN   SERVES:2

What You Need

- 250ml Almond Milk
- 100gm Frozen Spinach
- 1 Ripe Banana
- 1-Cup Ice Cube
- 1-Cup Chopped Frozen Green Apple

How To Cook

1. Blend everything and serve.

Nutritions

Calories 198 kcal, Carbs 44 g, Fat 1 g, Protein 4 g

Sauces and Dressing

45. Creamy Turmeric Dressing

 PREPARATION: 5 MIN   COOKING: 0 MIN   SERVES:6

What You Need

- ½ cup tahini
- ½ cup olive oil
- 2 tablespoons lemon juice
- 2 teaspoons honey
- Salt to taste
- A dash of black pepper

How To Cook

1   Mix all ingredients in a bowl until the mixture becomes creamy and smooth.

2   Store in lidded containers.

3   Put in the fridge until ready to use.

Nutritions

Calories 286, Fat 29g, Carbs 7g, Protein 4g, Fiber 2 g

46. Avocado Cilantro Detox Dressing

 PREPARATION: 5 MIN   COOKING: 0 MIN   SERVES: 3

What You Need

- 5 tablespoons lemon juice, freshly squeezed
- 1 clove of garlic, chopped
- 1 avocado, pitted and flesh scooped out
- 1 bunch cilantro, chopped
- ¼ teaspoon salt
- ¼ cup water

How To Cook

1. Place all ingredients in a food processor and pulse until well combined. Pulse until creamy.

2. Place in a lidded container and store in the fridge until ready to use.

3. Use on salads and sandwiches.

Nutritions

Calories 114, Fat 10 g, Carbs 8 g, Protein 2 g, Fiber 5 g

47. Easy Garlicky Cherry Tomato Sauce

PREPARATION: 5 MIN

COOKING: 25 MIN

SERVES: 4

What You Need

- ¼ cup extra virgin olive oil
- ¼ thinly sliced garlic cloves
- 2 pounds organic cherry tomatoes
- ½ teaspoon dried oregano
- 1 teaspoon coconut sugar
- ¼ cup chopped fresh basil
- 1 teaspoon salt

How To Cook

1 Heat oil in a large saucepan over medium heat. Sauté the garlic for a minute until fragrant.

2 Add in the cherry tomatoes and season with salt, oregano, coconut sugar, and fresh basil. Allow to simmer for 25 minutes until the tomatoes are soft and become a thick sauce.

3 Place in containers and store in the fridge until ready to use.

Nutritions

Calories 198, Fat 6 g, Carbs 37 g, Protein 3 g, Fiber 5 g

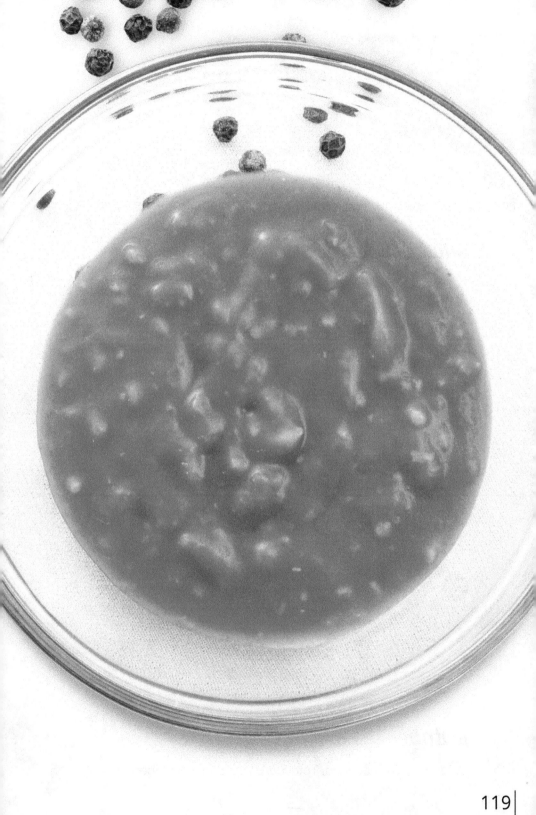

48. Garlic Ranch Dressing

 PREPARATION: 5 MIN   COOKING: 0 MIN   SERVES: 8

What You Need

- 1 cup nonfat plain greek yogurt
- 1 garlic clove, minced
- 2 tablespoons chopped, fresh chives
- ¼ cup chopped, fresh dill
- Zest of 1 lemon
- ½ teaspoon sea salt
- ⅛ teaspoon freshly cracked black pepper

How To Cook

1. In a small bowl, whisk together the yogurt, garlic, chives, dill, lemon zest, salt, and pepper.

2. Keep refrigerated in a tightly sealed container for up to 5 days.

Nutritions

Calories 17, Total Fat 0g, Total Carbs 3g, Sugar 2g, Fiber 0g, Protein 2g, Sodium 140mg

49. Peanut Sauce

 PREPARATION: 5 MIN    COOKING: 0 MIN   SERVES:8

What You Need

- 1 cup lite coconut milk
- ¼ cup creamy peanut butter
- ¼ cup freshly squeezed lime juice
- 3 garlic cloves, minced
- 2 tablespoons low-sodium soy sauce, or gluten-free soy sauce, or tamari
- 1 tablespoon grated fresh ginger

How To Cook

1 In a blender or food processor, process the coconut milk, peanut butter, lime juice, garlic, soy sauce, and ginger until smooth.

2 Keep refrigerated in a tightly sealed container for up to 5 days.

Nutritions

Calories 143, Total Fat 11g, Total Carbs 8g, Sugar 2g, Fiber 1g, Protein 6g, Sodium 533mg

50. Raspberry Vinaigrette

 PREPARATION: 5 MIN    COOKING: 0 MIN   SERVES:8

What You Need

- ¾ Cup extra-virgin olive oil
- ¼ cup apple cider vinegar
- ¼ cup fresh raspberries, crushed with the back of a spoon
- 3 garlic cloves, finely minced
- ½ teaspoon sea salt
- ⅛ teaspoon freshly ground black pepper

How To Cook

1 In a small bowl, whisk the olive oil, cider vinegar, raspberries, garlic, salt, and pepper

2 Keep refrigerated in a tightly sealed container for up to 5 days.

Nutritions

Calories 167, Total Fat 19g, Total Carbs <1g, Sugar 0g, Fiber 0g, Protein: <1g.   Sodium: 118mg

CPSIA information can be obtained
at www.ICGtesting.com
Printed in the USA
BVHW060439250321
603396BV00004B/266